By Kristi Yamaguchi

with Greg Brown

Illustrations by Doug Keith

Taylor Publishing
Dallas, Texas

Greg Brown has been involved in sports for thirty years as an athlete and award-winning sportswriter. Brown started his Positively For Kids series after being unable to find sports books for his own children that taught life lessons. He is the co-author of *John Elway: Comeback Kid*; *Scottie Pippen: Reach Higher*; *Dan Marino: First and Goal*; *Kerri Strug: Heart of Gold*; *Mo Vaughn: Follow Your Dreams*; *Steve Young: Forever Young*; *Bonnie Blair: A Winning Edge*; *Cal Ripken Jr.: Count Me In*; *Troy Aikman: Things Change*; *Kirby Puckett: Be the Best You Can Be*; and *Edgar Martinez: Patience Pays*. Brown regularly speaks at schools and can be reached at greg@PositivelyForKids.com. He lives in Bothell, Washington, with his wife, Stacy, and two children, Lauren and Benji.

Doug Keith provided the illustrations for the best-selling children's books *Things Change* by Troy Aikman, *Heart of Gold* by Kerri Strug, *Count Me In* by Cal Ripken Jr, *Forever Young* by Steve Young, *Reach Higher* by Scottie Pippen, and *Comeback Kid* by John Elway. His illustrations have appeared in national magazines such as *Sports Illustrated for Kids*, greeting cards, and books. Keith can be reached at his internet address: atozdk@aol.com.

All photos courtesy of Kristi Yamaguchi and her family unless otherwise noted.

Published by Taylor Publishing Company
1550 West Mockingbird Lane
Dallas, Texas 75235

Designed by David Timmons

Library of Congress Cataloging-in-Publication Data

Yamaguchi, Kristi.
      Always dream / by Kristi Yamaguchi with Greg Brown ; illustrations by Doug Keith.
            p.   cm.
      Summary: The young Japanese-American figure skater describes the hard work, determination and love of skating that helped her win a gold medal at the 1992 Olympics.
      ISBN 0-87833-996-5
      1. Yamaguchi, Kristi—Juvenile literature. 2. Skaters—United States—Biography—Juvenile literature. 3. Women skaters—United States—Biography—Juvenile literature. [1. Yamaguchi, Kristi. 2. Women skaters. 3. Ice skaters. 4. Women—Biography. 5. Japanese Americans—Biography.] I. Brown, Greg. II. Keith, Doug, ill. III. Title.
GV850.Y36Y36   1998
796.91'2'092—dc 21
[B]   97-49874
                                                              CIP
                                                               AC

Printed in the United States of America
10 9 8 7 6 5 4 3 2 1

Kristi, age 8

Hi! My name is Kristi Yamaguchi.

Growing up, I always dreamed of being a professional figure skater. After years of hard work, support from my family, and good coaching, I am living proof that dreams can come true.

Every day someone realizes a dream. I believe dreams help light our darkness and give us the push we need to move across the rink of life.

I've written this book to encourage you, no matter what happens, to always dream.

I've seen the world thanks to figure skating.

These days, I skate in about 70 American cities and several countries each year as a member of the Stars on Ice show and in professional competitions.

Being involved with sports has taught me many lessons. I know the frustration of falling short. Three times I finished second at the U.S. Nationals.

AMATEUR CAREER HIGHLIGHTS

1992	Winter Olympics–1st
	World Championships–1st
	U.S. Nationals–1st
1991	Trophée Lalique–2nd
	Skate America–2nd
	World Championships–1st
	U.S. Nationals–2nd
1990	Nations Cup–1st
	Skate America–1st
	Goodwill Games–1st
	World Championships–4th
	World Championships–5th (pairs)
	U.S. Nationals–1st (pairs)
	U.S. Nationals–2nd
1989	World Championships–6th
	U.S. Nationals–1st (pairs)
	U.S. Nationals–2nd
1988	U.S. Nationals–10th
	Skate America–3rd
1987	World Jr. Championships–1st
	World Jr. Pairs–1st

PAUL REID/IMG

And to this day I have not mastered the triple Axel jump, even after thousands of tries.

But I also know the joys of winning U.S. and world titles and Olympic gold.

Meeting people around the globe has taught me a simple truth: people are people. Despite our differences, we all have the same basic needs, feelings, and dreams.

PROFESSIONAL CAREER HIGHLIGHTS

1997	World Pro Championships–1st
	U.S. Pro Championships–1st
1996	Pro Skater of the Year
	World Pro Championships–1st
	Gold Championships–1st
	U.S. Pro Championships–1st
1995	Gold Championships–1st
1994	World Pro Championships–1st
	Gold Championships–1st
1993	World Pro Championships–2nd
	Challenge of Champions–1st
1992	World Pro Championships–1st
	Challenge of Champions–1st

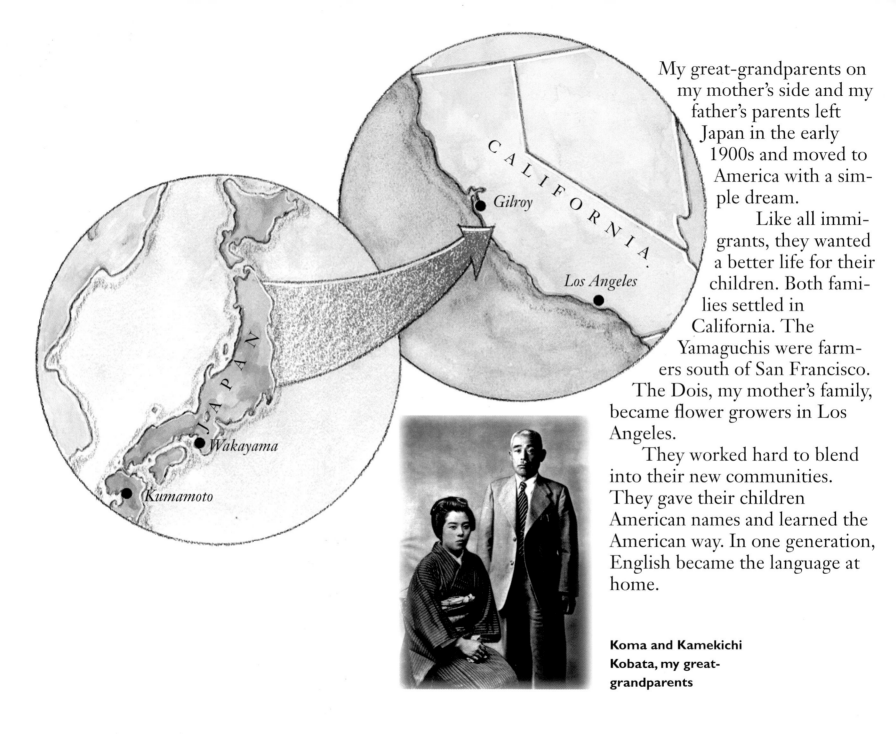

My great-grandparents on my mother's side and my father's parents left Japan in the early 1900s and moved to America with a simple dream.

Like all immigrants, they wanted a better life for their children. Both families settled in California. The Yamaguchis were farmers south of San Francisco. The Dois, my mother's family, became flower growers in Los Angeles.

They worked hard to blend into their new communities. They gave their children American names and learned the American way. In one generation, English became the language at home.

Koma and Kamekichi Kobata, my great-grandparents

Many families lost everything they could not carry.

Japanese-Americans endured many sacrifices to make it in America.

But they suffered most during World War II. Freedom and opportunity were taken from loyal West Coast Japanese-Americans soon after Japanese forces bombed Pearl Harbor, Hawaii, in 1941.

Fear of a mainland invasion made Japanese-Americans targets of anger and suspicion. It's hard to believe today, but the U.S. government stripped 110,000 Japanese-Americans of their civil rights by forcing them to live in ten "relocation centers" during the war. My father was five years old when his family was uprooted to Arizona. My mother was born in the Amache, Colorado, internment camp.

Ironically, my mother's father, George Doi, fought in Europe as an officer in the U.S. Army while his family was imprisoned back home.

Kathleen and George Doi, my mother's parents

LOOSE LIPS MIGHT Sink Ships

NATIONAL ARCHIVES

Dad's family was sent to this camp in Poston, Arizona.

In 1988 the U.S. government officially apologized for interning Japanese-Americans and issued a $20,000 check to each living survivor of the camps.

After the war, families rebuilt their lives. My parents grew up without being taught Japanese, and both went to college. My father became a dentist and met my mother, then a college student, on a blind date. They married and later settled in Fremont, California.

I came along as a middle child, two years after my sister, Lori, and three years before my brother, Brett. We were given Japanese middle names to remember our heritage. Mine is Tsuya (pronounced TSU-ya), my grandmother's name.

When I was born, on July 12, 1971, my parents immediately noticed something wrong with my feet—they were deformed, pointing inward and curling under. I wore casts and foot braces my first two years to correct the problem.

My parent's home in Fremont, where I grew up.

My casts were changed every two weeks. I teetered at first, yet I learned to balance and walk in casts.

My parents had a difficult balancing problem, too. They had to decide how to best incorporate two cultures under one roof.

We were taught and celebrated our Japanese heritage as far back as I can remember.

Still, we were a typical American family, and my parents tried to give us the best of both worlds.

Like our neighbors, we dressed up for Halloween, exchanged gifts at Christmas, and hunted for eggs at Easter.

I played basketball in a church league (Dad coached the team) and tried my hand at cheerleading.

My performing career started at about age four. Soon after the last set of casts came off, Mom enrolled me in dance classes as therapy for my feet.

That was fine with me. Lori already took ballet and tap. I wanted to be just like her. I even tried baton twirling lessons with Lori and performed in a parade. Lori went on to compete nationally in baton twirling and won a world title as a member of the Cruzers from San Jose.

I, however, quickly decided to quit twirling. Something else caught my interest.

Not far from my parents' house was an ice rink in the Southland Mall. There, local skaters would perform ice shows.

I remember seeing the glittery costumes, the dazzling spotlight, and their graceful movements. I wanted to try skating.

Mom thought skating might be dangerous for a four-year-old, so she said I'd have to wait.

We saw more ice shows, and I kept begging to skate.

"When you start school and can read, then we'll see," Mom promised.

I came home from my first day in first grade and announced: "I can read! Now can I go skating?"

Mom kept her promise. One day a neighbor who was my age and his mother agreed to go skating with Mom and me.

We rented skates. I had trouble standing, so Mom skated behind, holding me under my arms. We all laughed as we glided round and round.

When it came time to go home, I refused to give back the skates. I thought they were mine. It took awhile for me to understand the concept of rentals.

We rented skates several more times. Each time I asked for the same skates.

From that time on, I dreamed about skating in a professional ice show.

About that time Dorothy Hamill became famous by winning the Olympic gold medal in figure skating at the 1976 Games in Innsbruck, Austria.

I didn't understand what the Olympics were all about at the time. I just knew she had done something wonderful and that I had a connection with her.

I remember friends talking about Dorothy Hamill and saying, "Hey, Kristi, you ice skate, don't you?"

A few months later I received a Dorothy Hamill doll as a gift. I loved dolls. I had so many on my bed there was barely room for me to sleep.

"Dorothy" was special. I took her skating every day. Sometimes she sat on the edge of the rink and watched me practice, or I'd bring her on the ice and try to make her little skates run between my legs.

Soon I started taking group ice skating lessons, but it was far from a smooth start. I'd cry before class because going into a group scared me, especially if I had to skate across the rink or through other groups. Once classes started, however, I calmed down and was fine.

I progressed through various levels rapidly and gave my first ice performance at age seven.

Performing on ice came naturally, but I have always been shy and afraid to speak in group settings. I'd tremble at the thought of being called on by the teacher to answer a question I didn't know.

In junior high, being so short (I'm only 5-foot-1) had its disadvantages. Sometimes the taller kids would accidentally elbow me in the head as I walked through a crowded hallway.

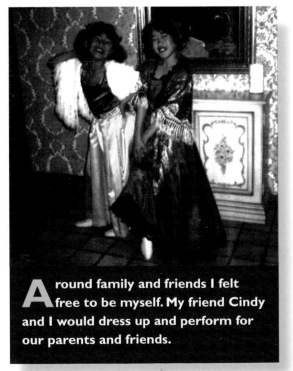

Around family and friends I felt free to be myself. My friend Cindy and I would dress up and perform for our parents and friends.

My most physically painful experience growing up happened the day I had ten teeth extracted. Six baby teeth and four permanent teeth were pulled by an oral surgeon in one sitting when I was nine.

My mouth was too small for all my teeth. So before I could have braces, room had to be made. Dad, who is a dentist, didn't want to hurt his little girl, so an oral surgeon removed the teeth.

I went in thinking, "This is no big deal." When I awoke, I thought I was dying it hurt so much.

Cotton balls on top of stitches gave me chipmunk cheeks for about a week.

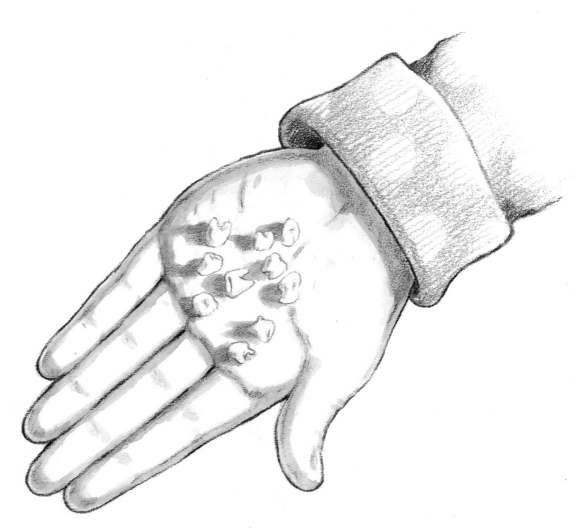

The only good thing about the experience was cashing in with the Tooth Fairy. We put all ten teeth in a plastic tube under my pillow. I found $10 under the pillow the next day.

I took two weeks off skating while my mouth healed. That's probably the longest I've been off the ice since.

One bad experience in a dentist chair didn't make me fear the dentist's office or dentists in general. I knew it was a one-time thing.

I had plenty of fears already.

My brother used to call me "Cricket." I don't know why—maybe because I'm terrified of insects, especially spiders.

My imagination runs wild

sometimes. I used to have many nightmares. My door had to be left open so I could hear the TV before I'd go to sleep.

Scary movies have always frightened me. Then, and now, when I see a terrifying scene, I'll put my hands in front of my eyes. Even *The Wizard of Oz* used to scare me (the flying monkeys and the Wicked Witch).

I refuse to watch any of the gory movies out there. I can't

handle it. Even some popular current movies give me trouble.

I shouldn't admit it, but I needed to cover my eyes and plug my ears during parts of *Jurassic Park*.

I remember two 12-year-olds sitting a row behind me in the theater laughing during the dinosaur attacks while I screamed.

One thing I've never been afraid of is competition. I get nervous, like everyone else, but never fearful.

That's because being on the ice has always been the one place I can truly express my emotions. The ice is like home.

I entered my first skating competition at age seven. When the winners were posted, my name topped the list.

Mom remembers my reaction to winning. She says I shrugged my shoulders and said, "Oh, that's nice."

For me, skating has never been about beating others. It's been about being my personal best.

Somehow, I knew early on that being my best meant putting in hours of practice.

I started training with Ann Cofer, my first personal coach, at age six. Two days a week, Mom and I would wake up early to fit in a couple hours of skating practice before school.

Ann gave me just what I needed—structure. She made me keep a log of each practice and write down everything I did.

Soon I started winning more local and regional competitions.

During a summer camp for skaters, I met one of the Bay Area's top skating coaches—Christy Kjarsgaard. She introduced herself by saying, "Hi, Kristi. My name is Christy, too."

That meeting led to other conversations about Christy being my full-time coach. Later, I began seriously training with Christy. I was nine years old.

Being coached by Christy meant a major commitment from my family and me.

Mom and I would wake up at 4 o'clock in the morning, six days a week. We'd drive across the Bay to be on the ice at 5 a.m. I'd skate for five hours. Mom often waited in the car or watched. Then I'd go to school.

The hardest part was going to bed when it was still light out. Waking up wasn't that tough. I wanted to get out of bed to learn more.

Every day Christy showed me exciting new things. I had mastered five of the six triple jumps by the time I was 14.

Coach Christy and I made a good team. I trusted and respected her judgment and advice. She respected my hard work. Christy has been my coach ever since. I still take lessons from her, even though I'm a professional.

I had another skating teammate in those early days. It was decided when I was 11 years old that I should also compete in pairs competitions with a talented young Bay Area skater named Rudy Galindo. Besides my morning skating, I'd meet with Rudy and pairs coach Jim Hulick for an hour after school.

Rudy and I skated together seven years. We grew up together and became like brother and sister. For a while, Rudy lived at our house as a member of the family, and we traveled the world together.

During my travels in the 1980s, I became fascinated by the Soviet athletes. In those days, the Soviet Union was seen as the Evil Empire.

I wanted to see for myself what was so different about these Soviet people. I reached out and befriended some Soviet skaters and learned to speak their language a little. Western blue jeans and makeup were in high demand in the Soviet Union, so those became our international language. Everyone wanted to trade for them. I'd bring free makeup samples from home, and Soviet skaters would trade me pins or clothing with the CCCP insignia.

Since the Soviet Union's collapse in the early 1990s, anything with CCCP lettering has become valuable to collectors.

Those exchanges with Soviet skaters taught me treasured lessons. I discovered that the Soviet skaters shared the same passion for skating I did. Once the labels, looks, and stereotypes are peeled away, we are all the same inside.

We're all the same, that is, except hockey players.

Figure skaters usually despise hockey players. First of all, hockey players take precious ice time away from us. The reason I had to get up so early every day was because hockey players hogged the ice in the afternoon.

Plus, everyone knows hockey players are gross. They spit all over the ice, they are violent, they change in the lobby, and their terrible stink after practice almost makes you sick just walking by them.

Dad and me at my high school graduation.

Thanks to skating, I had been around the world and a world champion by the time I was in high school. Rudy and I won the pairs gold medal at the 1987 World Junior Skating Championships, and I won the Junior Singles title.

Education was more important than titles in our family, though. I had to find creative ways to fit in school studies throughout my amateur career.

My junior high allowed me to have a flexible schedule, but the high school I was supposed to attended wouldn't allow my part-time schedule. I tried independent study for two years, but I felt too isolated. I found I needed to be around other kids my own age.

I attended Mission San Jose High, in Fremont, my junior and senior years.

Even though I didn't play a varsity sport, the school voted to award me a letter jacket after Rudy and I won the 1989 U.S. National Pairs title and I placed second in the '89 U.S. Ladies Singles competition.

That jacket meant a lot to me, and I wore it proudly at my first senior World Championships in Paris, France.

At a certain point in her career, the family focus was on Kristi. Still, she found time to show Brett and me that we were still important to her. I remember my senior cheerleader try-outs. She made a good-luck sign and came to the tryout to cheer me on. She never got too big for her family.
—Lori Yamaguchi

Twenty-four hours after graduating from high school, I moved to Edmonton, Canada. Coach Christy had married sports medicine doctor Andrew Ness and had moved there months before. Saying goodbye to my family and friends made me homesick before I left, but I knew deep down that I had to leave and train full-time to give my dreams a chance at reality.

I lived with Christy and her new husband for two years before moving into an apartment.

I trained in Canada from 1989 until 1994. Mom made periodic trips up to visit, which helped a lot, and I'd meet Rudy every few weeks, either in Canada or California, to practice our pairs routines.

Gramps always reminded us to work hard and to do our best. "Nobody can criticize you for that," he'd say. My grandparents tried to attend most of my competitions. They were my biggest fans.

The complications of distance eventually strained our pairs skating. Then, in late 1989,

Parents sometimes are a little too overzealous. When I said, "What happened?" Kristi broke down and said, "I wouldn't have fallen down on purpose!"

Sometimes we [parents] get caught up in the competition. Parents need to be calm and supportive and always show that we love our children unconditionally."—Carole Yamaguchi

I faced two death blows. Coach Hulick, at age 38, died of cancer that December. Five days later my grandfather, George Doi, passed away.

That was my first experience with deaths of loved ones. I cried for days and couldn't concentrate on skating. I knew, however, that neither would have wanted me to stop skating.

In Coach Hulick's memory, Rudy and I defended our U.S. Nationals pairs title in early 1990. But in singles I finished second again.

After a flawed performance in the long program, Mom asked, "What happened?" I burst into tears.

I did not skate well at the World Championships that year. Rudy and I took fifth, the best we could expect considering the competition. My fourth place in singles was disappointing to many people.

I felt pressure from all sides as many wondered if skating both singles and pairs was too much. My confidence cracked, and I considered quitting skating all together.

Finally, a choice had to be made—singles or pairs. It was like being forced to choose between a father or mother. I wanted both.

The choice was singles, for many reasons. Breaking up with Rudy was terribly sad—like a divorce in the family. We started so young together and had such great plans. But life doesn't always work out as planned.

Skating with Rudy taught me a different side of the sport, and I loved it. He made me a stronger skater. I wouldn't

trade our experiences together for anything.

I can understand that he felt left behind. I can only hope he understands my side. I'm proud of how he's bounced back and become a force in men's singles skating. Time has healed things between us. We're on friendly terms now.

Focusing on singles skating gave me renewed energy. I worked harder than ever.

Going into the 1991 U.S. Nationals, I allowed myself to believe I could win. But a third straight time I finished second. I skated tentatively, while Tonya Harding hit all of her triple jumps, including landing the first triple Axel by an American female.

It took me a good two weeks after that disappointment to pull myself together. I moped around at practice until four-time world champion Kurt Browning gave me some advice.

He practiced in the same Canadian rink and saw me going through the motions.

"Why are you doing this?" he asked one day.

"I don't know," I said. He then asked me to picture myself not skating at all.

"I love it. I can't stop," I mumbled.

"Then don't be afraid to smile once in awhile during training. Enjoy it!" he said.

My attitude changed, and the joy of skating returned. One month later, I skated one of my best performances and won the 1991 Ladies Singles World Championships.

Our American sweep in 1991 was a first in Ladies Singles World Championship history. Tonya Harding, left, was second and Nancy Kerrigan won the bronze medal.

It was just the boost I needed going into the 1992 Olympic year.

At the '92 Nationals I had another breakthrough with a gold medal. Still, going into the Olympics in Albertville, France, I was the underdog to Japan's Midori Ito.

Ito had mastered the triple Axel before Harding. Pre-Olympic media all focused on the Axel. Ito and Harding had it—I didn't. Could I win without it?

For 2 ½ years, 20–30 times a day, I tried the 3 ½ revolution triple Axel. Every time I fell or landed off-balance.

Sometimes it takes skaters months to learn a triple jump. The other triples (Salchow, Lutz, toe-loop, loop and flip) came quickly for me. I landed a triple Lutz the first day I tried it.

Sure, not landing the Axel frustrated me. But I didn't let it eat away at me.

I knew one jump wasn't going to win the Olympics. I had to perfect what I could do at the time and be happy with that.

I went to the Games with the attitude that I wanted to enjoy the Olympic spirit.

This might be hard to believe, but no one in my family, or Coach Christy, ever talked about me winning the gold medal.

In fact, I wouldn't allow myself to think about it. Some athletes visualize themselves winning gold. I was the opposite. I thought that would jinx me. I remember paging through a magazine before the Games and coming across a big picture of the medals. I instantly slammed the magazine shut without looking.

Because ladies skating didn't start until two weeks into the Games, some top skaters stayed away.

Not me. I attended the opening ceremonies, and I'm so glad I did. That's when you realize how big and special it is. I stayed in the Olympic Village and saw several other sporting events.

My practice sessions felt great leading up to the competition. Meanwhile, Ito, burdened with the expections of her country to be the first Japanese gold medalist, had been having trouble with her Axel in practice.

Finally, the day arrived. I felt the building tension for the short program. I remember stepping onto the ice and thinking, "I can't do this. How am I going to keep myself from freaking out?"

Then I remembered a note my choreographer, Sandra Bezic, had given me. It said: "This is your moment, let it shine."

I took a deep breath and eased into a solid performance that placed me first going into the finals.

Two days later I was the first of the final six skaters on the ice. Strangely, I wasn't as nervous. Just before I went on, Dorothy Hamill approached me and reminded me how hard I had worked and said, "Good luck! I'll be rooting for you."

Inspired, I glided onto the ice. Coming off the ice, I felt happy overall with my effort. I knew, however, that a slip had left the door open for someone else to win the gold.

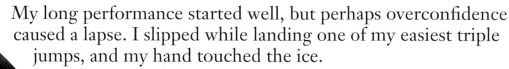

My long performance started well, but perhaps overconfidence caused a lapse. I slipped while landing one of my easiest triple jumps, and my hand touched the ice.

"I can't believe I just did that," I thought.

In a split second, for the first time in my career, I decided to change my planned program.

My next jump, the triple Salchow, had given me problems. I didn't want two mistakes in a row, so I did the jump with just two spins to play it safe.

As I neared the end, I had one more jump, the triple Lutz. "OK, this is it. You have to do this," I told myself. I landed it perfectly.

Then came the hard part—waiting for the others to skate. One by one, each made a major mistake. Ito and Harding both fell trying their triple Axels.

When medals were awarded, I found myself on the top step, the gold hanging around my neck and America's national anthem playing. Words can't describe the overwhelming mixture of emotions I felt.

Little did I know how much that one night would change my life.

Brian Boitano, a national, world, and Olympic champion from the Bay Area whom I admire greatly, sent me an e-mail that night with wise words of advice.

He said: "Don't do the party scene, don't think you're as good as people think you are, and be nice to people (even when you are having a bad day)."

I capped the season four weeks later with an emotional World Championships victory on my home ice in Oakland, California.

In a blink, a whirlwind of fame picked me up and spun my image around the world.

Interviews. TV shows. Magazine covers. Dignitaries. Celebrities. Parades. Fans. Endorsements. I had not prepared for this.

And I certainly had not prepared for questions about my heritage. The timing was ironic for me to be the first U.S. gold medalist in ladies figure skating since Hamill. Fifty years and two months after the Pearl Harbor bombing, during the height of economic Japan-bashing in America, there I stood, as *Sports Illustrated* put it on their magazine cover, an "American Dream."

Questions were raised about whether companies would ask me to endorse their products. "What are they talking about?" I thought. I'm American. I was born and raised in California. I have friends of all races. It bothered me that so much was made of it.

Looking back, all endorsement deals for athletes were down in 1992. I'll never know if some companies rejected me for being Asian. I signed my first deal—to endorse the fashions made by Celanese Acetate, a fiber company—two weeks after the Olympics and have been with them ever since. The people there have been loyal friends, and I feel like part of their company family. Over the years, I've had plenty of off-ice deals to keep me busy, including a fantasy line of skating clothing for young girls and a skating CD-ROM.

To me, skating has always been my motivation, not money. Endorsements are just icing on the ice.

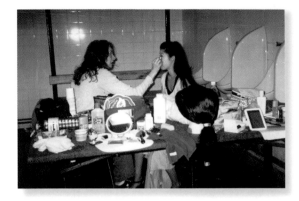

My big dream came true when I signed a contract to skate professionally with the Stars on Ice tour.

To skate with all the sport's stars is such an honor. The skaters and people behind the scenes embraced me into their family.

Suddenly, my structured life flip-flopped to road chaos. With Stars on Ice I travel five or six months a year. I thought life as a pro would be easy. It's not. It takes as much training now as before, and the travel is grueling.

We complain about carrying luggage, strange food, and homesickness. Still, when the lights go on and the crowd roars its welcome, there's no place we'd rather be.

My travel horror story happened in Brazil during my second year with Stars on Ice. We were in Sao Paulo on tour. Some skaters decided to go to the market before a show. On our way back, a group of bandits tried to stop our cars. Fortunately, we had a security force riding with us, and the robbers ran away unharmed.

OK, food on the road isn't all bad.

The goal of Stars on Ice is to celebrate skating and life.

We try to make the audience feel they are a part of every two-hour performance. In that spirit, Stars on Ice has joined the Make-A-Wish Foundation to brighten the days of children with life-threatening illnesses.

Throughout the tour, special children visit us at practice and sometimes have dinner with us. We develop relationships with these kids. Their courage in the face of incredible challenges teaches so much to all who meet them.

Those experiences helped me see that we all have the opportunity to make a difference in someone's life. Sometimes a random act of kindness or a word of encouragement is all someone needs.

But we can also help by giving to organizations. That's why I started the Always Dream Foundation.

Our goal is to make a positive difference in the lives of children. We do that with special fund-raising events, such as our annual Skates in the Park day in Golden Gate Park. The foundation supports various Bay Area organizations.

This is my special friend Angela.

The 1997 Skates in the Park event drew 1,700 skaters and raised $60,000.

Ekatarina and me at "A Celebration of a Life" for Sergei in 1996.

Scott and I skate a duet in tribute to Sergei.

On the road, the skaters and all the people behind the scenes develop a family bond. During the last few years we've realized the fact that terribly sad things sometimes happen to good families.

In 1995, pairs skater Sergei Grinkov, seemingly strong and in good health, collapsed on the ice during practice with his partner and wife, Ekaterina Gordeeva. Sergei died of a sudden heart attack.

That morning Sergei had given everyone a hug and flashed his warm smile. In an instant, he was taken away from his wife, his daughter, and us.

Ekaterina continues to skate in the tour and shows great strength. I gave her my heart earring as a sign of my support for her.

Then, in 1997, the heart of our tour, Scott Hamilton, left the show with an illness.

When he rejoined the tour, we learned he had cancer. Scott joked, "You can't get rid of me. Hey, I'm going to get through this. I'm going to be fine."

Later, he said, "The worst thing you can do in life is have a bad attitude."

Now, after receiving treatment and surgery, Scott's back on the ice, and the outlook is as positive as his attitude.

Scott stands 5-foot-3 because of a childhood growth problem, but he has a zest for life twice his size. He went on to become a four-time U.S. and world champion and an Olympic gold medalist. Now his battle with cancer is just one more reason why Scott Hamilton is a hero to me.

For other heroes in my life I need not look farther than my parents' front door.

What can I say to parents who love, support, and encourage me?

What can I say about a mother who gave up her career to keep me on the ice?

What can I say about a father who drove the same blue van for 20 years and spent thousands of dollars to see my dream come true?

What can I say about a sister and brother who, without jealously, have always been there for me?

What can I say to a family that never put me on a pedestal, that sees my faults, my grumpy moods, my down days, and still loves me?

What can I say? Saying "thank you" a million times would not be enough.

My family still loves me despite my inability to sing. I knew I couldn't carry a tune early on. Kids started laughing at parties when I'd sing "Happy Birthday."

I've become the singing joke on tour. When I sing, skaters and the crew will say, "Is that Barney?"

I'm pretty lousy at tennis and golf, too, but I still try. I also enjoy in-line skating, skiing, and surfing (on small waves).

Kristi has shown that if you stay dedicated and you have people's support, that's all you need.—Brett, Kristi's bother, who attends college and works for the Golden State Warriors

She's been able to handle fame and money because of her sense of family. She's successful as an athlete and a person because of the morals that have been instilled.—Lori, Kristi's sister, an events coordinator in the Bay Area

We never pushed her into skating. We said as long as she was having fun we'd support her.—Jim, Kristi's dad

I really admire and respect the woman that Kristi has become. Away from the ice, she has remained thoughtful and giving of herself and has taken charge to remember those not as fortunate as herself.—Carole, Kristi's mom

My family

One of my most memorable days was visiting the Osaka City Sports Center for disabled children. They inspired me with their joy and hope, regardless of their physical limitations.

I am also thankful for my heritage. Without it I wouldn't be who I am.

I learned to appreciate it more in 1994, when I visited Japan with a Goodwill delegation from Northern California. I had skated in Japan before but never had the chance to stop and meet the people and my relatives.

We attended receptions in Osaka, Kyoto, and Tokyo—all planned down to the minute—during the 10-day trip. I also spent time with my mother's family in Wakayama.

The trip took me full circle. I started to understand why we did certain things in our family and could appreciate the values passed down by generations.

It made me see that countries and races don't make history—people make history.

Like it or not, we are all connected hand-in-hand to the past. We complete each other's stories. Learning your own family history helps you better understand yourself.

HEINZ KLUETMEIER/IMG

Kristi with the Stars on Ice cast.

I hope to start a family of my own some day and pass on that connection to the past.

For now, skating makes even having a boyfriend difficult. Over the years Mom and I have argued most about who I date. Imagine her surprise when I told her I was dating a professional hockey player!

We met at the Olympics and became friends when his team crossed paths with our tour. Who would have guessed a hockey player and figure skater could be happy together?

I don't know what will happen with us. We are both in the middle of our time-demanding careers. In a way, the ice is still our first love.

How can anyone love ice? Frozen water can be so painfully hard and oh so cold—just as life can be. Ice doesn't care who skates across its surface. It doesn't care who loses balance and falls on its slippery back.

Still, for me, the ice is a warm world of beauty and grace—a place of complete freedom to express my emotions. Being on the ice is being alive.

As you glide your way along life, my suggestions are to pursue the things that make you feel alive and to remember: Always Dream.